Channels (France)

Habitats
(*Habitations*)

by Philippe Minyana
translated by Steve Waters
from a literal translation by Christopher Campbell

Habitats was first read in the UK, in this
translation, at the Lyttelton Theatre on
26 June 2002.

The reading was directed by Fiona Laird.

TRANSFORMATION

29 April–21 September 2002

The Lyttelton *Transformation* project is vital to my idea of the National Theatre because it both celebrates and challenges our identity. What do we want the National to be? We must draw on our heritage, on our recent past, and on the talent of the next generation. I want a thriving new audience, including a body of young people under 30 with a theatre-going habit, a new generation of artistic and administrative talent committed to taking the National forward and a realization of the varied potential within this glorious building.

Trevor Nunn Director of the National Theatre

Transformation is thirteen world premieres, hosted in two new theatre spaces, with special low ticket prices. The National's most traditional auditorium, the Lyttelton, has been transformed by a sweep of seats from circle to stage to create a new intimacy between actor and audience. At the same time the Loft has been created – a fully flexible 100-seat theatre. *Transformation* will introduce new generations of theatre makers and theatre audiences to one of the most exciting theatres in the world.

Mick Gordon Artistic Associate
Joseph Smith Associate Producer

Transformation has received major creative input from the Studio – the National Theatre's laboratory for new work and its engine room for new writing – and celebrates the Studio's continuing investment in theatre makers.

NATIONAL THEATRE STUDIO & TRANSFORMATION

All the plays in the LOFT and the *Channels (France)* readings are co-produced with the National Theatre Studio. The Studio is the National's laboratory for research and development, providing a workspace outside the confines of the rehearsal room and stage, where artists can experiment and develop their skills.

As part of its training for artists there is an on-going programme of classes, workshops, seminars, courses and masterclasses. Residencies have also been held in Edinburgh, Vilnius, Belfast and South Africa, enabling artists from a wider community to share and exchange experiences.

Central to the Studio's work is a commitment to new writing. The development and support of writers is demonstrated through play readings, workshops, short-term attachments, bursaries and sessions with senior writers. Work developed at the Studio continually reaches audiences throughout the country and overseas, on radio, film and television as well as at the National and other theatres.

SPRINGBOARDS – a series of partnerships created by the Royal National Theatre Studio with other theatres, enabling work by emerging writers to reach a wider audience – provided a platform for new writing and translation with a series of co-productions which have included Zinnie Harris' *Further than the Furthest Thing*, Gregory Burke's *Gagarin Way*, Richard Bean's *Mr England*, and the *Remembering the Future* season with the Gate Theatre.

DIRECT ACTION, a collaboration initiated in 2001 between The Studio and the Young Vic, focuses on providing young directors with an opportunity to work on the main stages, as did Rufus Norris with David Rudkin's *Afore Night Come*, and Gregory Thompson with Max Frisch's *Andorra*.

Since 2000 a new strand of International Projects, including the CHANNELS initiative, has allowed the Studio to become a regular partner in collaborations and exchanges across the world: in France, Argentina, Lithuania, Italy, and in the Balkans.

For the Royal National Theatre Studio

HEAD OF STUDIO Sue Higginson
STUDIO MANAGER Matt Strevens
TECHNICAL MANAGER Eddie Keogh
INTERNATIONAL PROJECTS MANAGER Philippe Le Moine
RESIDENT DIRECTOR (LOFT) Paul Miller

CHANNELS (FRANCE)

The *Channels* translation initiative aims to establish bridges between plays and playwrights across Europe and beyond. Its development began at the NT Studio in January 2000. *Channels* not only provides opportunities for new plays to be translated into – as well as from – the English language, it also allows for a direct and creative exchange between playwrights, translators, dramaturgs, directors and ultimately with the audience.

The cornerstone of all *Channels* projects is the Residency. This is the crucial phase when writers and translators can work hand-in-hand. It also provides unique moments when playwrights from different horizons can exchange emotions, compare practices, get a view on other dramatic worlds and reflect on their own.

Channels began with France: five British writers were given a first opportunity to tackle contemporary translation, and five French writers have been translated in the UK for the first time. We are delighted that these five plays are being given a first public reading on the Lyttelton stage as part of the *Transformation* season and that Oberon Books have shown their trust and enthusiasm in the project by giving the texts a chance to reach audiences beyond the Lyttelton.

Channels has opened up possibilities for long-term collaborations with partners in Europe and especially in France where it coincided with the launch of the House of European Contemporary Writing (aka M.E.E.C.). Three British plays – Richard Bean's *The Mentalists*, Gregory Burke's *Gagarin Way* and Mark Ravenhill's *Mother Clap's Molly House* – were translated into French and read at the Studio of the Comédie Française in February 2002. Two new *Channels* projects are currently being set up with Argentina and with the Balkans. *Channels* has been enthusiastically supported by all the participants and has set a new pattern for translation initiatives. It has proven a unique approach for entering someone else's culture and for laying the foundations of further exchanges.

Partners and supporters include: the French Theatre Season Awards, the French Embassy in London, the Burgess programme, The French Institute in the United Kingdom, the S.A.C.D. (Entr'Actes), the British Council Paris, the A.F.A.A., the Mousson d'Eté festival and M.E.E.C. (House of European Contemporary Writing), and Oberon Books (London). Thanks to the literal translators and the readers: Chris Campbell, Philippe Le Moine, Rachael McGill, Simon Taylor and François Raffenaud. Special thanks to Véronique Bellegarde.

PHILIPPE MINYANA

Philippe Minyana has written over fifteen plays since 1980 including: *Le Dîner de Lina*, *Fin d'été à Baccarat*, *Chambres*, *Inventaires*, *Les Guerriers*, *Où vas-tu Jérémie?* and *Commentaires*. He has a long working relationship with Robert Cantarella who has staged most of his plays. Many of them have been translated and produced abroad. He has also worked with musicians such as Georges Aperghis. In 1999, some of his plays were included in the French curriculum for the Baccalauréat. His most recent works include *Portraits* (Théâtre Ouvert, 1999), *Habitations* (Théâtre Ouvert, 2000).

STEVE WATERS

Steve Waters' plays include *Anarchy in UK* (Birmingham Allardyce Nicholl Studio), *Utopians* (Birmingham Allardyce Nicholl Studio, Pegasus Theatre, Red Room Theatre), *Growing Up Stupid*, *Italy Year Zero*, *English Journeys* (Hampstead Theatre, New Directions Season), *After The Gods*, *London Bridge* (Paines Plough Wild Lunch season at the Bridewell).

CHANNELS (FRANCE) 2002

Wednesday 12 June
Presentation and launch of the series at the Institut Français, South Kensington

A series of rehearsed readings in the Lyttelton Theatre:

Friday 14 June, 2.30pm
RISING BLUE
by Jean-Paul Wenzel (2000)
translated by Lin Coghlan
Reading directed by Deborah Bruce

Wednesday 19 June, 2.30pm
BATTLE OF WILL
by Laurent Gaudé (1999)
translated by David Greig
Reading directed by John Tiffany

Friday 21 June, 2.30pm
HILDA
by Marie NDiaye (1999)
translated by Sarah Woods
Reading directed by Dalia Ibelhauptaite

Wednesday 26 June, 2.30pm
HABITATS
by Philippe Minyana (2001)
translated by Steve Waters
Reading directed by Fiona Laird

Friday 28 June, 2.30pm
LE PUB!
by Serge Valletti (1998)
translated by Richard Bean
Reading directed by Mick Gordon

All readings are followed by informal meetings with the playwrights, translators and directors.

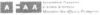

The chief aims of the National, under the direction of Trevor Nunn, are to present a diverse repertoire, embracing classic, new and neglected plays; to present these plays to the very highest standards; and to give audiences a wide choice.

All kinds of other events and services are on offer – short early-evening Platform performances; work for children and education work; free live entertainment both inside and outdoors at holiday times; exhibitions; live foyer music; backstage tours; bookshops; plenty of places to eat and drink; and easy car-parking. The nearby Studio acts as a resource for research and development for actors, writers and directors.

We send productions on tour, both in this country and abroad, and do all we can, through ticket-pricing, to make the NT accessible to everyone.

The National's home on the South Bank, opened in 1976, contains three separate theatres: the Olivier, the Lyttelton, and the Cottesloe and – during *Transformation* – a fourth: the Loft. The building is open to the public all day, six days a week, fifty-two weeks a year. Stage by Stage – an exhibition on the NT's history, can be seen in the Olivier Gallery.

TRANSFORMATION SEASON

IN THE LYTTELTON

A co-production between the National Theatre & Théâtre National de Chaillot

The PowerBook .... 9 May–4 June
from a novel by Jeanette Winterson
devised by Jeanette Winterson, Deborah Warner & Fiona Shaw
Director Deborah Warner

A Prayer for Owen Meany .... 10–29 June
a novel by John Irving
adapted by Simon Bent
Director Mick Gordon

A collaboration between the National Theatre & Trestle Theatre Company

The Adventures of the Stoneheads .... 4–13 July
written & directed by Toby Wilsher

A collaboration between the National Theatre & Mamaloucos Circus

The Birds .... 22 July–3 August
by Aristophanes, in a new version by Sean O'Brien
Director Kathryn Hunter

Play Without Words .... 20 August–14 September
devised & directed by Matthew Bourne

IN THE LOFT

Sing Yer Heart Out for the Lads .... 29 April–15 May
by Roy Williams
Director Simon Usher

Free .... 20 May–8 June
by Simon Bowen
Director Thea Sharrock

Life After Life .... 28 May–8 June
a reportage play by Paul Jepson & Tony Parker
Director Paul Jepson

The Shadow of a Boy .... 13–29 June
by Gary Owen
Director Erica Whyman

The Mentalists .... 4–20 July
by Richard Bean
Director Sean Holmes

Sanctuary .... 25 July–10 August
by Tanika Gupta
Director Hettie Macdonald

The Associate .... 15–31 August
by Simon Bent
Director Paul Miller

Closing Time .... 4–21 September
by Owen McCafferty
Director James Kerr

HABITATS

First published in English in 2002 by Oberon Books Ltd.
(incorporating Absolute Classics)
521 Caledonian Road, London N7 9RH
Tel: 020 7607 3637 / Fax: 020 7607 3629
e-mail: oberon.books@btinternet.com

A catalogue record for this book is available from the British Library.

ISBN: 978-1-84002-310-7

Characters

NARRATOR(S)

EXECUTIVE

VOICE

BROTHER

COLLEAGUE

EMPLOYEE

ACTRESS

YOUNGER MAN

OLDER MAN

Prelude

Slide projections of kitsch idylls. A NARRATOR speaks.

1

NARRATOR: You make out Elizabeth's smile through the twitch in Elizabeth's cheeks.

2

NARRATOR: Thornton Rust – Jennifer, Peter, Bob, Avril and little Peter laze about on deckchairs on the bijou patio having pigged out on gammon utterly confounded in thought.

3

NARRATOR: Anthony says to me he hasn't got his act together but he's about to get it sorted.

4

NARRATOR: Skellingthorpe, dining room – conversation gives way to mastication at which point Angela suddenly blurts out God it's fabulous here and everyone laughs.

5

NARRATOR: Hayley insists she's never had a holiday this good what with thermals on wooded ridges and the non-calorific snacks rustled up for her personally by Mrs Mummery.

6

NARRATOR: The epiphany came about six one evening
after a swim Jackie and Jake munching grapes stunned
by the notion that the mere transformation of where
they were would have a concomitant effect on their
outlook to the extent that they could firmly affirm they
were free utterly free of everything.

7

NARRATOR: There was a peace a sort of respite suddenly
Paul and John were hit by the fact that the very air they
inhaled was the open air.

8

NARRATOR: Mary-Anne giggled non-stop until about
five it didn't suit her I have to say she has this freakish
giggle stinking of cities but deep in her heart one
might detect sheer unabashed joy at the good fortune of
being permitted to reside at Walton on the Naze.

9

NARRATOR: The quasi-Moorish villa had some good
points namely that it made them insane with gaiety.

10

NARRATOR: Annabel scurries into her cosy bungalow to
nibble fruitcake calmly life unfolds serene.

11

NARRATOR: Marjory rose with the dawn the sea calm
nothing yet astir and astonishingly she sensed she'd live

for 102 years which shocked her so much she sang a
song.

12

NARRATOR: Elizabeth who can't abide her folks holidays
with them at her gramp's house in Stubbers Green.

13

NARRATOR: Jackie states she adores the palm tree arbour
Jake claims it makes him gloomy Jackie exclaims
Florence is a magnificent place Jake rejoins he doesn't
care for Florence much and Jackie asks herself why
Jake always asserts the polar opposite of what he thinks.

14

NARRATOR: Thornton Rust – Jennifer Peter Bob Avril
and little Peter nap but Jimmy the dog yaps and they
wake with a start.

15

NARRATOR: The sprinkler refreshes Annabel's
herbaceous borders which are in fine fettle a fact for
which she thanks her lucky stars.

16

NARRATOR: Thornton Rust – Jimmy the dog scratches
himself mum and dad have gone for an amble my
brothers play badminton and I wait for whatever.

17

NARRATOR: Anthony informs me that on a walking tour of Barcelona he slipped on a scrap of sticky paper which marred his stay in Barcelona.

18

NARRATOR: Hayley who lives in Hull informs me that sometimes on the streets say mid-January it's as if you've stepped outside of time itself.

19

NARRATOR: Matlock – Anthony says he's crawling up the walls I say why not accompany me to Wookey Hole he says no chance he has to sweat this depression out.

20

NARRATOR: Thomas Bernhard writes somewhere that the human voice is by and large unbearable.

21

NARRATOR: Hayley informs me that Mrs Mummery's mildly smelly hair is forcing her to rethink her association with Mrs Mummery.

22

NARRATOR: Anthony writes to me that sea-swimming has opened him up a bit.

23

NARRATOR: Jonathan told Margaret that she was cursed
with an intolerable tendency to be holier-than-thou she
stopped dead in her tracks saying I'll go and pick those
plums but in fact she went for a cry in the shed but
other than this mishap all proceeds to plan at St
Clethers everyone on tenterhooks agog for Mary-
Anne's return from Basingstoke full of modish theories
and since the rain began we've all been hunkered down
in the living room I expect we look a bit glum it has to
be said that leaving aside Colin's witticisms there's a
collective malaise compounded by little Sophie's
saying she's fed up happily Caroline who has a knack
of saving the day has volunteered to man the cooker
and rustle us up a mixed grill.

24

NARRATOR: In the garden – Jennifer offers Avril a
cutting from her purple rose redolent of the grave –
Avril who can't stomach the stench of lilacs bursts into
tears.

25

NARRATOR: St Stephen's Coombe – Jake writes that
Jackie's insufferable qualities make her indispensable
he goes further stating that without Jackie he couldn't
go on he is somewhat taken with Sadie who apparently
observed this to him he admits he's a capricious bugger
claiming to despise his mother for her ceaseless fussing.

26

NARRATOR: We rented a holiday chalet on the Isle of Skye which reeked of milk our stay was ruined.

27

NARRATOR: Torremolinos – John and Mary had to abandon the quasi-Moorish villa thanks to its owner Senora Sarfati of the lank grey hair hurling kitchen waste at them it's not so much the kitchen waste that did it Mary confessed to me as the degeneration of Senora Sarfati who is completely gaga and John chipped in that the quasi-Moorish villa had an unsettling air to it.

28

NARRATOR: Biggleswade – Anthony reprimands me for my absurdly apocalyptic tone citing instead the need to address dumbing-down I demanded what he meant to which he replied take a look around you can't you see the grotesque vulgarity of everything.

29

NARRATOR: Annabel surveys the par-terre she is obscurely sad she eats an artichoke and two chocolate drops goes to the lounger and mellows.

30

NARRATOR: Chingford Mount – Susan is a straightforward soul inhabiting a carefree world the cares of others puzzle her having arranged for herself a life of impeccable discipline.

31

NARRATOR: Margaret writes to me that following a catastrophic holiday she's a vacant dead thing.

32

NARRATOR: Sidi-Boussaid – Marjorie writes the following to me what I cherish is the endless time of Sundays nothing to be done but to read in bed or to sit in your robe on the settee now and again looking up at the foliage shuddering in the breeze.

33

NARRATOR: Hutton-le-Hole – I phone my cousin Geoffrey who says to me I'm on crutches this cow stampeded me other than that everyone's alright.

34

NARRATOR: Margaret writes to me I go to pot in winter indifferent as to whether anyone might desire me having got out of the habit of desire and I've got to be a chubby little thing I don't recognise.

35

NARRATOR: Queen Elizabeth Way – Anthony tells me he's under self-imposed house arrest in his own home I say why not join us in the Malverns?

36

NARRATOR: My sister calls me up to say my husband spends his life behind a screen we laugh we hang up and I think of mother dead in her prime.

37

NARRATOR: Elizabeth informs me that after her dad died they sold off Stubbers Green and broke her heart I suggest she move on.

38

NARRATOR: Julie says she's as low as a cow or as high as a flea as ever Julie's all over the shop.

39

NARRATOR: Paul and John write they could hole up for months on end in this place of livestock flies evening mists pines and pretty lady-bakers.

40

NARRATOR: The cherries are on their tree the gravel on the drive and all's right with the world.

41

NARRATOR: Cioran writes: 'If things were called by their proper names no form of society would last a second,' and quotes Queen Christina, 'the secret of happiness lies in rejecting everything.'

42

NARRATOR: Symonds Yat – Paul and John write that they love every second of the day but the early mornings are hard my throat tightens writes one I'm afloat in happiness the other.

43

NARRATOR: Hayley writes to me that she thirsts for conversation because words can be cathartic but after fifteen minutes on the coach with Mrs Mummery she blurted you're a stupid little soft-toy to which Mrs Mummery replied you've betrayed me but there we are it's to be expected because finally we all betray one another.

44

NARRATOR: My sister tells me anything is better than stagnation even a shriek and a knife I say what are you saying?

45

NARRATOR: A philosopher once said, 'Frightened of being one thing or another I've ended up being nothing.'

46

NARRATOR: Anthony writes to me that his life is a write-off.

47

NARRATOR: Sheerness – my sister writes to me that her Christian upbringing drags her into the depths going on if I only knew what my problem is going further I hurt right now.

48

NARRATOR: Elizabeth who's doing her place up asks me my feelings about granite ceramics I tell her I don't rate them I think I've upset Elizabeth.

49

NARRATOR: Brittany – I walked on the path that overlooks the port leading through scrub to the beach the birds sang the church bells tolled it was perfect.

50

NARRATOR: As soon as Marjory got home she planted poplars.

Habitats One:
The Executive, The Voice

1

The EXECUTIVE stands smiling. Silence. As nothing happens he reads out a fax.

EXECUTIVE: (*Reads.*) Fax from a Mr Percival of FAS Co.: 'It takes skill to create made-to-measure and mail-order systems. In an increasingly competitive environment with a more demanding customer base rapid delivery is of the essence. Implementing your theories of added value generation has facilitated our just-in-time stock capacity and total security product delivery; who profits? – the client. My global quotation incorporates packaging and logo-usage.'

The EXECUTIVE waits. Silence. As nothing happens he reads out another fax.

Fax from a Mr Gawain of EXO Concerns: 'It's certainly made-to-measure for which many thanks and the polyurethane foam achieves outstanding performance levels; maximum protection, minimum weight. Many thanks for facilitating the streamlining of our marketing and express delivery systems.'

Slide projection of a town.

Hey – that's Plymouth!

Another slide of a younger man representing the EXECUTIVE. It doesn't look like him.

VOICE: (*Off.*) Are you the chap in the picture?

EXECUTIVE: Sure.

Slide goes.

VOICE: (*Off.*) You're from Plymouth then?

EXECUTIVE: Yep.

Slide projection of advertising material. 'Question: What do the following have in common? An Aeroturbine, a PC and a Ming Dynasty Vase.'

Always been in PACKAGING.

More slides of adverts for Packaging systems. The EXECUTIVE reads under his breath the text.

'PAK EXPRESS – high speed quotations, Twenty-Four-Seven –
Guaranteed two hour turnaround after we get your call. You have our TOTAL assurance of COMPLETE protection to fit your PRODUCTS.
PAK EXPRESS – because your needs are our needs.
PAK IN PLACE FORMATS –
In under forty-eight hours we deliver to your door bespoke packaging within one metre accuracy –
with the same EXCELLENCE of PAK-EXPRESS at your leisure.
PAK IN PLACE – because where you are is where you need us.'
Born in Plymouth studied in Hull, always been in PACKAGING.

The EXECUTIVE laughs and reads a notice shown on a slide.

One. Space Efficiency: dual carton.
Two. Better Protection: wipeout repair costs.
Three. Labour Efficiency.
Four. Slashed Transport Costs: low-weight foam
massively reduces bulk and casing size.

Slides of publicity for Pak-Sell and Pak-Away; as before
EXECUTIVE mutters text quickly.

'PAK-AWAY – you're one quick phone call away from
units designed for your products MADE JUST FOR
YOU – whatever the need, speed or distance we get
there first.'

Slides of two images of small boys: one represents the
EXECUTIVE (that is, the actor); the other is any old photo.

VOICE: (*Off.*) That you in that photo?

EXECUTIVE: Sure.

Two slides of young men intended to represent the
EXECUTIVE. Neither looks like him.

VOICE: (*Off.*) That you in the photos?

EXECUTIVE: Surely.

Images of Advertising Copy. Text: 'Packaging Systems
Moulded In Situ.' The EXECUTIVE reads a caption linked
to the images.

'Packaging Systems Moulded In Situ.
One. Conforming with Safety Specification.
Two. Less Bulky: dual carton.
Three. Easy-Fit.
Four. Easy-Maintenance.'

So what exactly do we mean by Maintenance? In a word it's the core sector of business that facilitates the on-going functioning of the process.

'Five. Guaranteed Moulding Quality.'

End of images; the EXECUTIVE adds.

Polyurethane tops polystyrene any day.

The EXECUTIVE, smiling, waits. An image of a town.

Hey – it's Plymouth.

End of image. The EXECUTIVE, smiling, waits. The VOICE coughs a few times. Silence.

VOICE: (*Off.*) We hear you Mr Papagueno, we hear what you're saying.

EXECUTIVE: Okay, good, good, lovely.

The EXECUTIVE reads out a fax.

Fax from a Mr Chum, from ChumCorps: 'With our high-sensitivity electro-calibration scales we need to ensure our client base will get regular deliveries in total security set-ups. Thanks to you we've met client demands and fulfilled our mission statement.'

The VOICE coughs. The EXECUTIVE smiles happily.

2

The EXECUTIVE waits smiling.

One or more slides of a young man apparently representing Executive's BROTHER. These may be of a lightly disguised actor, or of someone else altogether. Immediately we hear the Voice of the Executive's BROTHER (who shares his brother's voice and therefore can be played by the same actor). The BROTHER speaks more quickly. During the BROTHER's monologue, the EXECUTIVE laughs and slaps his thighs saying the following statements a number of times: 'That's my brother from Marfleet. We're in packaging the pair of us.'

BROTHER: (*Voice off.*) I deliver your empty computer boxes which IBM use to stick computers in after hmm repairs and return via special delivery so hmm I cut down their in-house man-hours boost their service quality post-repairs cos it's pretty arsey to do a quick fix, quick bodge pack, quick hmm drop-off and then get em back bollocksed again hmm seeing as we're locked into an IBM guarantee maintenance process hmm but then your IBM hmm here again it's a question of judgement sure I shell out at the packaging end but then you got your costs when the thing gets to the hmm bollocksed again hmm put bluntly it's unworkable what I always say hmm I don't sell foam or casing no I put on the market a practical hmm convenient solution hmm and there's market niche for it we're drawing up the same package for Toshiba hmm with Toshiba hmm we said right we deliver the empty boxes to your hmm to Daventry and hmm in go the what monitor mouse keyboard accessories so hmm they assemble little 'bundles' yeah sort of clumps and it's hmm your IT kit but for logistic constraints they get screens from Taiwan keyboards from Spain hmm and end up with our packaging gunk under their feet for couple of weeks occupying premium space I said to them for God's sake send your info stuff to me here and before the week's out I'll have fifty-two pallets with mice screens monitors the works I'll get your Bultex to order stop you from falling in same shit Toshiba were in hmm six months back ah got the packaging but just not the hmm mouse so I can't hmm or the keyboards not got them they got stuck at customs in Germany so I can't hmm but you know myself once I've got the works Geronimo get the bundles sorted (*Small pause.*) stick the lot in casing seal it up get transport cartons and whack it out to hmm Toshiba's clients thereby completely annihilating the bid starting with the bespoke packaging hmm polyurethane foam again for hmm hmm maximum delicacy you got to remember some of the kit in those bundles is extremely fragile.

Slide of a town.

EXECUTIVE: Hey, that's Plymouth!

Slide off. The EXECUTIVE waits, smiling. Slide of publicity copy. The EXECUTIVE reads the accompanying text.

'One. Get Sorted. Simplified bespoke service.
Two. Get Flexible. The right solution for your way of pricing and working.
Three. Get Costs down. One-stop control of direct and indirect costs.'

The EXECUTIVE looks at the copy slide and smiles several times.

'Just in Time.'

Slide off.

The EXECUTIVE waits, smiling. Several slides of young men seen in rural settings. One is an image of the EXECUTIVE, the others don't resemble him.

VOICE: (*Off.*) That you in the snaps?

EXECUTIVE: Of course.

EXECUTIVE reads a fax out.

Fax from a Mr Krook of BRET: 'Since we went into partnership, my firm feels reborn; many thanks.'

The EXECUTIVE smiles happily. He continues.

'Since we merged with the world leader in polyurethane foam injection we can guarantee maintenance and delivery of primary products.'

The EXECUTIVE adds, stressing each syllable.

So in a word what is maintenance? As I said it's none other than that sector of a firm's activities that facilitates its continuance in operational mode. And as my little brother says, we're making available on the market a practical, convenient solution.

3

The EXECUTIVE waits, smiling. A couple of slides representing Executive's COLLEAGUE; could be the actor disguised or someone else; almost immediately we hear the COLLEAGUE's voice (either the actor's or another's). During the COLLEAGUE's monologue, the EXECUTIVE laughs, slaps his thighs and says several times: 'That's my colleague alright.'

COLLEAGUE: (*Voice off.*) We packed up some paving-slabs (*Coughs.*) which were bound for Sweden for examination by Scientists who wanted to check-out these paving-slabs (*Coughs.*) these paving-slabs (*Coughs.*) would they split or not split under freezing conditions (*Coughs.*) see if they could withstand British road repairs (*Coughs.*) the key thing (*Coughs.*) here was that the slabs got to Sweden in peak condition (*Coughs.*) right? So for these tests on Swedish roads thirty-odd British paving-slabs were despatched to Sweden to get tested there get tested they're being tested we've just secured a deal on isothermic containers for labs which carry vaccines in sealed dry-ice cryogenic casings stabilising product conditions for say two three day deliveries so your vaccine is (*Coughs.*) our isothermic packaging is still your basic polyurethane in a variant formula yeah differential mass of foam of forty kilo your actual sealed cell foam I mean these vaccines are geared for Argentinian livestock right (*Coughs.*) and if your vaccines turn up and they're dickey you've got a bovine epidemic on your hands (*Coughs.*) we're highly constrained by massive value add-ons market forces cos cos this sealed cell foam casing is highly complex in the manufacture (*Coughs.*) takes an hour minimum to determine foam functioning (*Coughs.*) I mean this is a relatively pricey product but then it's all relative cos you've got your cost-benefits Argentinian livestock going (*Coughs.*) so your vaccine's kept at very low temperatures for two-three days in a process which we worked out from our own internal thermo-testings (*Coughs.*) which at the end of the day is the bottom line.

Projections of stereotypical baby snaps.

VOICE: (*Off.*) Pictures of you?

EXECUTIVE: Sure.

Image of a town.

Oh great – Plymouth.

End projections.

VOICE: (*Off.*) You were in Balls Green after Plymouth, yes? Balls Green, right?

Silence.

EXECUTIVE: I know nothing about Balls Green.

VOICE: (*Off.*) So what comes after Balls Green?

Silence.

What comes after Balls Green?

Silence.

VOICE: (*Off.*) Then it's, what, Uxbridge, right?

EXECUTIVE: Yes. Uxbridge. Okay.

Image of EXECUTIVE in Uxbridge.

VOICE: (*Off.*) That a photo of you then?

EXECUTIVE: Absolutely.

4

Silence. The VOICE coughs a few times. EXECUTIVE speaks quietly, during which the VOICE coughs a few times.

EXECUTIVE: I have my two hats my logistics hat and my packaging hat and I do my utmost to get across to the hauliers get your clients to opt for different packaging regime you gain from an upgraded brand and your client gets fewer breakages in the bargain blah blah so I slightly fall between two stools but right now the hauliers aren't set up for it cos cos essentially they're shit-for-brains yeah shit-for-brains real shit-for-brains totally but you got to y'know make the effort to lay down the law with your hauliers but then again they have other concerns and it's an advisory capacity at bottom advisory yeah that's right advisory you say you've got your client there you giving him twenty-two per cent breakages you got to ask is that dodgy transport or packaging? You know it's one or the other could be both yeah both and ninety per cent of the time it's poor initial packaging ninety per cent of punters consider good packaging to stick a printer in foam chips or bubblewrap stick it in a cardboard box hoik it over to your courier it's a common misconception in packaging that your foam-chips and bubblewrap give zero shock-absorption whereas technically speaking polystyrene can take one tumble but not two and as we're talking express-couriers if there's loading-slippage your parcel falls right there on your platform at Uxbridge falls in loading-slippage on the Manchester flight falls in baggage-handling turns up at Mansfield no hang on not Mansfield Macclesfield twelve hours later that's five consecutive falls with polystyrene at one-fall absorption only and thereafter we're technically speaking write-offs cos it's one-fall absorption max.

The VOICE coughs.

5

The EXECUTIVE stands smiling.

Projection of young man (one or more) intended to represent the EMPLOYEE. Could be the actor in make-up or someone else. Almost immediately we hear the EMPLOYEE's voice which could be the actor's voice or another's.

The EMPLOYEE speaks slightly slowly; during his speech the EXECUTIVE laughs, slaps his thigh and says a few times: 'Yep that's my employee alright!'

The sound of a workshop.

EMPLOYEE: (*Voice off.*) Stage one mould manufacture showing in reverse product outline stage two inject in the mould polyurethane foam expanding to fill mould in twenty-two seconds stage three extract a sort of sponge spongey-thingy that's the premould roughly showing the form of the product intended for transportation that's the lot.

6

The EXECUTIVE speaks quietly.

EXECUTIVE: It has to be admitted that Transport Culture is not ready for this breakthrough granted they have their own headaches running transport which is in the end their chief concern and then you've got the Packagers who are not running with it either and yes it is a leap in the dark, the unknown a quantitative step forward from flogging cardboard which can only compete on price your cardboard comes in at a quid okay ninety-eight p. okay I can take it off you for that price even if we sell it at a mark-up there's always cost constraints sure but you have to think this one through you know and say fine I grant you cost constraints but what about your costs when it turns up fucked again cos you have your quid's worth of packaging and these are real figures these are are are your current trade rates in this field quid's worth of packaging one smash in every two three quid one in twenty not one in twenty which is a bad percentage but one actual smash in a hundred one per cent breakages alas you can't allow for a monitor in your average driver-drop-off so even then you get the odd smash no getting away from it so here we are in this gaping hole in the market offering a

whole range of services like let's say you want some
furniture sent overseas yeah say to the States Canada
the item collected at an antique-dealer you've picked it
up as it comes so we do the packaging here not
necessarily with foam maybe another process which we
tailor to the given transport-methodology cos the said
item's headed for Canada in a container-ship it's a
wardrobe okay you can hardly carry it over no we're
not talking bloke with parcel we're talking pallet
ensuring the need for blockage/stalling surface
protection from state-of-the-art shock-absorption
RandD so I reckon pallet – cardboard-box –
bubblewrap yeahyeahyeah finishing touch cardboard
sealed pallet some massive fork-lift jobby (*Gestures to
indicate largeness.*) fork-lift lifts up the hoiks up the the
your your cupboard into the container-ship slapped
down in the hold and that's your lot so we aren't
talking foam given the item is 1200 by 40 deep, 930
height gonna end up on a pallet in a box anti-scratch
protection from duolene from bubble-wrap little lateral
strips of PU that's polyurethane foam protection I
mean polyurethane's all over got it in footwear
polyurethane padding course it's petroleum-based
there's numerous formulae yielding liquid or solid
forms whatever so we're slotting little strips in cos as I
said we're not talking man with parcel here pick-it-up
and there you are we're talking crane-lift into container
fifteen days at sea there you go and right now you don't
get your offers your antique-dealer calls transport-outfit
says I've got this wardrobe needs shifting to Canada
guy saying I'll take it off your hands get it to Canada
but you sort the packing I aint a packer or arse-about
say your packagers saying wait a sec sir I package said
item but can't offer delivery right whereas we are prime

positioned with this foolproof offer I subcontract out to a courier good worker dead reliable knows the carrying gen on such-like items cos there are flybynight boys in this trade oh yeah you get your cowboys alright so we go for the expensive courier but then it's all relative in the final analysis yeah yeah cowboys alright so he gets the said item here in safety locates a partner for the Canada drop-off I give my client a global solution that's what he gets for his money transport packaging and pick-up costs my mark-up end of story.

7

Projections of the Uxbridge works with the EXECUTIVE and the EMPLOYEE in action.

VOICE: (*Off.*) So what sort of stuff do you generally deliver?

EXECUTIVE: (*Quietly.*) PCs, Ming vases, turbines, (*He pauses, pretends to think.*) missile warhead turbines.

8

Projections of EXECUTIVE swirling and pirhouetting; most images show the actor, some another actor.

VOICE: (*Far away.*) That you in the pictures there?

EXECUTIVE: Of course.

Habitats Two:
The Actress, The Younger Man, The Older Man

The ACTRESS takes a small text from her bag. Recites as if in school. The two MEN listen.

ACTRESS: 'I stand amidst men as Jesus of Nazareth calling for his sleeping disciples.' Schopenhauer.

Puts the book away. Sniffs. Pause. Takes it out again. Opens it and recites as if in school.

'The present alone is true. It is time filled up. There alone our being dwells.' Schopenhauer.

Clears her throat several times. Recites.

'Time is within us, unfolding without obstacle.' Schopenhauer.

Sniffs. Puts book down. Long pause.

Human beings are gawping bull seals with horribly hard lives.

Sniffs several times.

Human beings are beer-swilling marionettes.

Reopens books and recites.

'At times when we feel nostalgia for some faraway place we are in fact nostalgic for the days when we lived in that place for then we were young and fresh.' Schopenhauer.

Puts book down. Smiles a few times.

There was a time when I got estranged from everything couldn't name anything anybody around me I felt like I was wobbling the bit that kills you's always at the outset yes at the very outset.

Pause.

And looking sideways always sideways like I was so full-up with tears I was scared any moment they might – flow.

Pause.

And infancy was horrifying you come out of the egg and wham.

Short quick slide-show. Places from the ACTRESS' childhood: a house with terrace, hallways, garden, trees – palms, figs, pets.

What keeps you from drowning tea at four or the sound of the sea –

Pause.

Either way it's not mother-love or the finger of God.

Pause. ACTRESS takes a note-book from her bag.

My notebook.

Opens it and reads out.

'The scene could take place near a lake a hill any sort of relief to enhance the comeandgo of wind and light speaking for a lake its pluspoints blind us to the inevitable lassitude of its shore blotting out the key idea before us nullity nothingness.'

To the two men.

That work for you?

The YOUNGER MAN laughs. No reaction from the OLDER MAN.

'Actually the scene takes place by the sea which is worse for it devours all that is imaginable so much so that one is defined by the phrase "ah you live by the sea".'

Stops. Indicates she is omitting a paragraph.

'However when still and clear the sea is so divine it makes one yearn for death the happy face of death the part one craves when savouring the taste of things on the tongue.'

Stops, closes the notebook, smiles a few times, pauses. A quick sequence of slides; faces – the ACTRESS's family, with the ACTRESS.

We lived for a time with my mother's mother my mother having wanted to break with her mother had a wall built in her mother's house exactly like the Berlin wall this was 1954 and granny reduced to tears by the wall was only permitted to cross the wall at Christmas there was a door within the wall my mother who was insane retained the key and when granny slept in the evenings we traversed the wall the bedrooms being upstairs and in the morning my granny would linger in her bed until we had traversed back through the wall before settling in her tiny spot as we had to traverse this tiny spot in order to reach the bedrooms and in the wing of the house where we lived isolated from granny there was a kitchen a living-room and basement toilets that we shared with granny mother told me her mother could never stand her and also with her mother's mother the same scenario hatred being hereditary and then mother got her cancer and father who'd turned a deaf ear went blind.

To OLDER MAN.

It's painful looking at you it's always painful looking at those close to you who are leaving it's always painful looking at people who are close to you.

To both men.

You're listening to me feeling utterly alone they listen to you eyebrow raised lips half parted and you say screwdriver when you should say armchair and do they twitch even actually actually they weren't even listening.

To OLDER MAN.

And when you're away from me I think of you as I would a corpse absent-minded theatrical.

Pause.

Surely I loved you long enough.

Pause.

(You see a face you love it but it's only the memory of another face it reminds you of which fools you into thinking you love the owner of the face in actual fact you've lost sight of the owner having gotten fixated on a detail end of story.)

The ACTRESS completely still. Apparently distracted, asleep. Long pause.

39

Once more down the long corridors of oblivion the long corridors of oblivion is that clichéd?

The YOUNGER MAN purses his lips in perplexity. The ACTRESS goes up to the YOUNGER MAN and claps her hands by his face, frequently. She laughs and sits.

'Nothing's more unfathomable than happiness.'

To the OLDER MAN.

Yes yes I have your manuscript.

Takes the manuscript from her bag and reads from it at random.

'Halliday: They said you didn't want to see me.
   Pause.
   Do you want to see me?
   Pause.
   You seem faraway.

'Dietrich: Aunty's collapsed the hussars have come.
   Halliday sits.
No you don't do that when you come here you
   telephone first.
   Pause.
   You know I'm living under tight surveillance that I
   tolerate it all for the sea swimming I reckoned I
   didn't go for swimming in the sea but I adore it to
   the point of madness I'll never cease to regret living
   here it takes no time at all to ruin a life Aunty says
   to me cherub I'm as lonely as an old soft-centre at
   the bottom of the chocolate-box one voice says get
   out of here another says give it time.'

She stops reading the manuscript, clears her throat a few times.

Okay so you've borne fruit.

No response from the OLDER MAN.

You've borne fruit.

OLDER MAN still silent. She opens her bag, puts manuscript away. Takes several texts from the bag and shoves them into the YOUNGER MAN's hands.

Have my old Penguin first editions, my Pelicans, there.

The YOUNGER MAN takes the books embarrassedly.

YOUNGER MAN: Thanks very much.

The ACTRESS notices a stain on her clothes.

ACTRESS: Grotty old food mark.

Scratches at stain with her nail.

Takes me back to the egg-yoke on the blouse episode I was in *André's* with that filly the one who likes to be known as Iris the anorexic and she's gawping at my blouse and then goes and flicks egg on it staining me and it hit me right then that I could never again be at peace with anybody in the world this business with the stain dredged up all the old hurts opened the scabs so I said get back in your rabbit-hutch you stupid stupid cow and Iris said yes yes it's all my fault yes so I said to her well let's bloody well see a few tears then.

To the two men.

Are your rags all stained?

The YOUNGER MAN examines his clothes for stains.

It'll all fall in place when you work out there's no purity none all thanks to Original Sin which screws everything up for all time just a bit of yoke on my blouse and I'm shattered life is totally totally unbearable.

The YOUNGER MAN has found a stain and cries out.

What's the nature of your stain, then?

YOUNGER MAN: Ketchup.

Long low laugh from ACTRESS.

ACTRESS: There's someone behind the door.

She goes to look; no one; she acts as if really scared, does a number.

Some days you don't know if you can take it you see everything you do like it was already memory you open your mouth hear your voice say to yourself hey that's my voice go all feeble or stir yourself even get close to praying at times.

The YOUNGER MAN laughs a bit; he's understood she needs a listener and signs of response. The ACTRESS is on a roll. Does another number, strokes the men's wrists, then her own, then the backs of their necks then her cheeks.

So smooth. Just so smooth. Miraculous.

She acts without interruption an extract from 'Happy Days' by Beckett, Winnie, her briefcase taking the role of Winnie's handbag.

'And yet it is perhaps a little too soon for my song. (*Pause.*) To sing too soon is a great mistake, I find. (*Turning towards bag.*) There is of course the bag.

(*Looking at bag.*) The bag. (*Back front.*) Could I
enumerate its contents? (*Pause.*) No. (*Pause.*) Could I, if
some kind person were to come along and ask, What
all have you got in that big black bag, Winnie? give an
exhaustive answer? (*Pause.*) No. (*Pause.*) The depths in
particular, who knows what treasures. (*Pause.*) What
comforts. (*Turns to look at bag.*) Yes, there is the bag.
(*Back front.*) But something tells me, Do not overdo the
bag, Winnie, make use of it of course, let it help
you…along, when stuck by all means, but cast your
mind forward, Winnie, to the time when words must
fail –' (*She closes eyes, pauses, opens eyes.*)

*The ACTRESS has ceased acting, she goes to the OLDER
MAN (still silent, static) shows him her forehead and lips
several times.*

Wrecked forehead lips sour past repair.

No response from OLDER MAN. To YOUNGER MAN.

And the house burnt down a real blaze granny in
flames and we moved in with my Aunt who limps they
operated on her but went too far with the bone work
and now she limps on the other side a pathetic freak
my father's sister my brother the eldest an apprentice
had his first attack so they put him in the Home
twenty-one years of age Mum was recalled to the
Uterus Clinic my blind father would go out driving
with an illiterate boy who couldn't decode road signs
policemen would drop them back home this world-class
Soprano friend of Mum's Pepita Sanchez came round
and sang a bit which was a saving grace the limping
Aunt who slept with her son made a play for father her
brother that is bathing his feet his hair his genitals in
the dining room which she soon stopped when mum

43

got back from the Uterus clinic and Pepita Sanchez
came round and sang again which was still a saving
grace and my cousin the limping aunt's son planned to
strangle his mother my aunt because one night in the
bed they shared she allegedly tried to have sexual
intercourse with him which I don't in fact believe my
brother the eldest was released from the Home but he
didn't have any hair he helped out with my aunt's small
business my father who'd had an operation on his eyes
could only see out of the one and my limping aunt's
husband the barber tried to rape a small girl and was
arrested and my brother the eldest who used to shout
out loud all the time for no good reason was returned
to the Home we didn't get to see much more of my
brother who looks like a Roman Emperor who has my
mum's looks who looks like an Empress who says I
look like an old dry prune and then we were bankrupt
father having made some questionable deals and we
were fed by my limping aunt on the proceeds of her
small business.

*And without interruption the ACTRESS performs an extract
from the last act of Chekhov's 'The Seagull'.*

'I am so exhausted. Sleep…sleep…they mocked my
dreams so much I've given them up, I too have lost my
courage… Then the torments of love, jealousy,
constantly fearing for my little one. I was becoming
mean, paltry.'

She dries. She gestures that she will continue.

'Since I came here I walk a lot, I walk and think
deeply.'

She dries again. Makes the same gesture.

'The essential thing is to know how to endure. To learn to bear your cross and hold to your creed. I have faith and suffer less, and when I remember my calling, life has no fears for me. Tsk. I'm going. Farewell.'

She gestures as before to indicate she is omitting lines.

'Its late. I can barely stay upright... I'm shattered...I'm starving...no, no don't come with me, I'll go by myself. My troika is hard by.'

Same gesture.

'Men, lions, spiders, silent fish, denizens of the waters, starfish, and those invisible to the naked eye, in a word all life is extinguished having run its sad course. For millennia, nothing has lived upon the earth and the poor moon lights her lantern in vain. In the fields, cranes awake no more with a cry, one hears no longer the sound of a cockchafer in the lime groves.' There – bang on.

She laughs, behaves like a little girl, jumping for joy. The YOUNGER MAN laughs as well. She takes his arm and they both jump for joy. The OLDER MAN remains silent. She stops abruptly.

'Dear sis, looking at the sea makes me think of our past together the sea makes me think of our past together the seasons mean nothing to me as I am tenderly cared for I feel like a tiny lizard on a tiny branch.'

She puts the letter away and recites.

'In the last analysis all life swings between the will-to-attain and that which is attained. Desire, in essence, is pain. If one attains what one desires, one is swiftly sated: the attainable desire was mere appearance; once attained, this desire has no charms. Thus desire takes a new form and a need ensues. In its absence, the desert, vacancy, *ennui*.'

The YOUNGER MAN sighs a lot.

You're on the brink of the abyss.

YOUNGER MAN: I await the descent of serenity.

(Short pause.)

If it can in fact descend.

The ACTRESS pulls the skin of her face in all directions, a game which she rather prolongs; the YOUNGER MAN, embarrassed, laughs.

ACTRESS: If your soul is damaged settle for less perhaps a dead flower tossed in the bin nothing but a dead bloom wham in that bin and then you're in tune with the universe in with the rubbish where you belong.

Pause. She laughs.

In the manor's grounds down in the dead grass Mrs Mills arse over tit – sixish dusk shitty sky and what do I espy but Mrs Mills under grey turrets grey towers down in the grass I spy Mrs Mills hitting the bottle.

Pause.

And I sing a song.

Sings.

'Will I always remain
A wretch and a waif
No hope nor home
After one day giving way

46

Slipping into the unknown
Finding shelter of a sort
Finding food on the hoof
With soul-sisters of a sort
Who offer a good look to all
Knickers removed
Skid-marks and below
What did we do to deserve
To fall so far –'

Small pause.

The Council evicted Mrs
Mills I didn't make any fuss
I should have done
as a young woman I joined various
associations which had reunions
you brought soft drinks along
if you went to the loo
when you returned someone would have
swiped your soft drink not the ones who'd
bothered to bring their own of course
no just the cheats and the bad seed.

The ACTRESS swiftly gets some papers from her briefcase.

A text by my dear friend Marcel Scholenko.

She reads quickly.

'In Penge the other day I encountered this Neanderthal
musing on the universe with his prick hanging out a
prick so hard and thin it could barely function qua
prick I entered into the revery of the Neanderthal
whose face was white as the proverbial sheet having
recently lost everything after the collapse of a futile
course of study in Data Programming I reminded him

that in Eden his ancestor Adam had also in the course
of a single day lost everything becoming the source of
a veritable chain reaction of calamity and I went
further indicating his prick Behold the Digit of Disaster
it was the time of day when if one's left alone one
either sleeps or tops oneself he collapsed in the bushes
and dozed whilst I became preoccupied with the image
of the body as the tomb of the soul and as night drew
to a close and the birds sang and the skies temporarily
trembled I shivered with a kind of ecstasy.'

She stops reading.

Script by Marcel Scholenko who was shot dead he used
to be a director.

She takes letters and postcards from her briefcase.

Marcel Scholenko who adored me wrote this to me:
'How well I know that I resist the inevitable and
despise the fatuity of this rage this heat naturally I'm
aware there are matters of greater import I refer to you
my darling ah if I only I could be just utterly adrift in
our love.'

She reads another letter.

This as well: 'My dear, after a tricky passage (winds
refusing to blow in the correct direction) docked at
Guernsey and visited the house of Victor Hugo which
is hateful and nauseatingly rococo although view from
first floor very fine have started sleeping once more
after wretched insomnia but not regained land-legs and
walk as if in drunken stupor which is tiresome as
seasickness. Life on board confined ache to see you
once more I thirst once more to love you Marcel.'

She takes a postcard.

'Kisses from Crete an immersion bath for body and soul swim every day.'

She takes another letter.

This as well: 'I never knew until now how the absence of tenderness renders life lethal.'

She takes a postcard.

This too: 'Prospect of Martinique discovered by Columbus in 1502 area 1080km square temperate climate all year round I'd forgotten the meaning of joy.'

The OLDER MAN gets up and leaves. ACTRESS and YOUNGER MAN watch him go.

He's gone.

Pause. She grabs another letter.

This as well: 'Miss you monotonously in the daytime and savagely at night leaves me sleepless makes me feel old and useless.'

She puts the letters and cards away carefully, as the YOUNGER MAN opens his own briefcase.

YOUNGER MAN: I wrote a play and sent it to Radio 4 and this was their response:

'Dear Sir, Please find enclosed copy of your returned MS "Ameria Shelter". Sadly I am not in a position to offer a positive response to the submission which received a unanimously negative reaction from the reading panel who were revolted by it.'

He stops, laughs loudly, slaps his thigh etc. then recommences reading.

Blahdiblahdiblahdiblahdiblah.

Reads end of letter.

'Hopefully next time I will be able to respond to a different play from you which will elicit a different reception yours sincerely et cetera.'

He stops, laughs, slaps his thighs, takes the manuscript, offers it to the ACTRESS who opens it and reads.

ACTRESS: 'Stage directions: setting: Imaginary country well not absolutely imaginary as it's definitely set in the Middle East where dirty deeds are a matter of course where hidden struggles aren't very hidden and the fall of a woman –'

Pause.

'– functions as the defining image of this country okay let's say this Middle Eastern country she herself being the most striking expression of it but this country let's characterise as Middle Eastern is only a decoy as you could easily imagine we're in some other country and therefore not in the Middle East as such but on another landmass where in much the same manner anything is permissible and conflicts hidden or otherwise secure the insidious destruction of our cherished aims.'

YOUNGER MAN: Actually I went there after I read an in-depth supplement in *The Independent* twenty-eighth February 1995 what hit me hardest in this in-depth supplement was a picture with the caption, 'Ameria Shelter' this shelter destroyed by two US missiles where a woman'd been living yes inside the shelter ever

since the bombing not going out of the shelter and in
the supplement there were two reports one titled, 'Iraq
Refuses to Ratify ninety-three Convention,' the other,
'Chemical/Biological Weapons Used as a Deterrent
Against the Poor,' alleging that chemical weapons are
being manufactured from products virtually on the
open market describing vesicular combat gasses like
say mustard gas which attacks the respiratory tracts
destroys skin cells saying that toxins used for warfare
work like a sort of biological arsenal like those poisons
which take out the digestive tract causing death by
septicaemia toxaemia –

ACTRESS: What?

YOUNGER MAN: Tox-aem-ia – blood poisoning – tox-
aem-ia –

ACTRESS: (*Reads.*) 'Scene One:
The Woman: Here at Ameria Shelter
    this was where we came it was 3:30 pm
    they said hurry up
    we're going in there
    In the shelter
    We went into the shelter and there were eleven
    thousand casualties
    And since then the shelter became well known –'

Pause.

So this was a war.

    'And BLAMBLAM the two warheads
    And it was ashes and dying people
    Screaming
    And I didn't know my own
    When a face is eyeless when eyes
    are closed it is a different face

51

And ashes covered faces
And in a second I became widow and orphan
On account of the death of my parents
My husband's death
My children, their deaths also
And I couldn't speak I was only tears
But I couldn't weep these tears
The warheads took everything from me even my
tears
I moved amongst the dead
My dead the dead of others
And my voice called out
Despite it all called out
And my head said be quiet but my mouth was
unable to –'

She stops reading.

When I visited the detached house I said to the chap
from the estate agents I want to buy this detached
house I go inside the detached house and wow I'm like
head over heels the very next day I call the chap in the
estate agents and demand he show me round I go right
into the detached house I see this man the inhabitant
drinking a cup of coffee he slumps he's dead I say to
the chap from the estate agents he just died drinking a
cup of coffee there knob of butter slices of bread his
effects in an adjoining room an unmade bed all
untouched the chap from the estate agents told me the
daughter adored her dad and hadn't touched a thing
couldn't bring herself to does that bother you dirty
dishes festering leftovers I say to the chap from the
estate agents this is a house full of ghosts he says yes
his wife died shortly before him I saw the dead in there
as in the Ameria Shelter.

She indicates the YOUNGER MAN's manuscript.

And the man and woman lead one another to death
cheek by jowl fifty years of mutual loathing sure but
neither one capable of lasting alone and when the first
one goes the other shortly follows in the garden flowers
everywhere I thought how wonderful to die amongst
flowers because my thought was that once I owned it I
would die there in the detached house I lived part of
my life in the detached house and to my surprise I
didn't die there so I sold the detached house I couldn't
abide it any more you shouldn't spend your whole life
in your house.

Pause.

My mother hated my father she let herself die quite a
solution she cooked up to leave him she stopped
feeding herself according to the neighbour Mrs
Merchandise who saw her every day of the fortnight
preceding her demise she was acutely sensitive in her
feelings in the words of Mrs Merchandise she suffered a
paroxysm of hatred to quote Mrs Merchandise who
gave her a good shake insisted she should eat
something and actually she was secretly eating sardines
in oil according to Mrs Merchandise who called the
doctor who suggested Father go away for a brief period
while she regained her senses Father said he had no
idea where to go so he stayed put and Mother resolved
to die she hung herself but the cord snapped in the
mean time Mrs Merchandise gave her another good
shake and made her some soup but Mother said she
couldn't stop herself death was the only solution how
can I live without it she said to Mrs Merchandise and
she said she'd had a bellyfull of life Father told the

homehelp to locate all the ropes on the premises and burn them but Mother had hidden away a good thick hemp and hung herself with it but it snapped as well but this time the drop ensued in a fatal blow to the skull in the words of Mrs Merchandise and Mother was left comatose and when Father phoned me it was already finished she'd hit the jackpot in the words of Mrs Merchandise.

Pause.

You know my brother the one that looks like an emperor he writes me these little poems now.

She takes some papers from briefcase. Reads.

'I watch the apple tree an apple falls and me I just wait.'

Pause. Takes another paper.

'What else can I do in my den other than wait for that perfect time in the morning or the evening or in the mists when ancient miracles get born or reborn daytime or night-time the beautiful possibilities get born and you seek and seek a soul mate who says to you here I am how long can you hold out for the hope of warmth care the hope of two living as one.'

Small pause. The OLDER MAN returns. An exchange of glances.

Habitats Three: Narrator(s)

1

NARRATOR comments on a photo.

NARRATOR: 'Vestibule of the Manor,' photographed by
James Inwood.

Audience may or may not see image.

Claire before the door in skirt, cardigan door of oak
glass lights dark lacquered trim to left interior wall
adjacent the wall a study area floored with ceramic
tiles.

James' vision: 'I saw Claire lying dead in the vestibule,'
observation recorded during infamous trial.

In the vestibule left five cupboards ceiling overhauled
front door comprised of numerous leaded lights light
glitters in the vestibule the whole disposition of the
vestibule provides the period-effect manor with a warm
ambience.

2

NARRATOR comments on photo.

NARRATOR: 'The Arbour,' photographed by James
Inwood.

Audience may or may not see image.

The pitched pine roof extends out into an arbour-like
covered passage of stripped pine which adorns not

merely the interior of the manor but extends to the exterior beneath and beyond the porch's awning most of manor's rooms protrude gabled Claire in cargo pants and pullover supervises the children's swimming in the kidney bean shaped pool with a face of panic the handrail running alongside the steps into the porch is weather-proofed oak.

3

NARRATOR comments on photo.

NARRATOR: 'The Master Bedroom,' photographed by James Inwood.

Audience may or may not see the photo.

Claire in nightwear laid-out on bed hair tied into bunches the bedroom bisected by partition one side bedroom proper other side ensuite bathroom brushed stainless steel fittings.

Charlotte posing in bathroom holding towel printed with the face of Winnie the Pooh the much-loved character attributed to A A Milne Charlotte looks at her mother who looks out of the window.

4

NARRATOR comments on the photo.

NARRATOR: 'The Children's Bedrooms,' photographed by James Inwood.

Audience may or may not see the photo.

As is standard throughout the property the children's rooms are furnished with sliding French windows which offer quick access to the arbour stripped pine floor surface light throughout matching furnishings.

James' vision: 'I see my wife and children lying dead in their beds.' Observation submitted as evidence during infamous trial.

Responding to Prosecution's query, the Expert Witness replied that he was not suffering from dementia at the point of the events.

Question from the Prosecution recorded during the infamous trial: 'Did you suffer from cancer yes or no?'

'James Inwood chokes back dry tears,' Press comment.

James' journal, submitted as documentary evidence during the infamous trial: 'Key thing is waterproofing of roof lining tiles up sealing off surface below tiles gutters to be kept unblocked not forget checking of joints around chimney skylight examine roof-frame tap with mallet all areas rotten parts give hollow sound auscultate frame with stethoscope detect inevitable insect presence.

'But how to find inner calm.

'Don't forget wire-wool for perfect insulation.

'Certainly got my work cut out.'

Letter from Claire's mother to Claire submitted as evidence during infamous trial: 'I frankly consider the manor to be an act of folly where will you get the capital your Father tells me he's entrusted our savings to James whom he claims has a good head for business.'

Letter from Claire to Mother submitted as evidence during infamous trial: 'Stop fussing mum James's got a handle on things the house is a haven of peace.'

Letter from Mother to Claire submitted as evidence during infamous trial: 'I'm afraid I continue to harbour grave misgivings about you-know-who he's so naive well we'll see what we see.'

Letter from Claire to Mother submitted as evidence during infamous trial: 'Yesterday we picked fresh mushrooms everything's fine.'

Letter from James Inwood to his lover Sadie Jestice submitted as evidence during infamous trial: 'Meet you at Windsor Great Park can't wait for it I'm choking.'

5

NARRATOR comments on the photo.

NARRATOR: 'The Kitchen,' photographed by James Inwood.

Audience may or may not see the photo.

Alternating façades of white laminate and stainless steel minimise linearity just as kitchen cupboards surfaced in enameled caramel and mouse-grey sandstone combine wrought iron hood of modernised Aga to form a unity of architectural interest granite-like coated work surfaces in U-shaped configuration the kitchen provides a capacious area facing the dining room with built-in sink ensuring the hostess need not turn her back on her guests.

6

NARRATOR: James' vision. Observation submitted as evidence during infamous trial: 'The dog lay dead in the field.'

7

NARRATOR: Medical report. Read out during infamous trial: 'Bristol Radcliffe Infirmary; Department of Cardio-Vascular Investigations. Effort-test of Mr James Inwood: Negative.

'Method: Ergometric Bicycle: Energy produced start: thirty watts; climax: 150 watts; total effort time: thirteen minutes.

'Results: Functioning signals: none. Reason for stopping: effective muscular exhaustion.

'Comments: Sub-maximal effort test negative. Coronary weakness highly improbable. No arrhythmia. Functional capacity: satisfactory.'

Evidence of family doctor, Dr Labrador submitted during infamous trial.

Question from the Prosecution: 'Was he ill, yes or no?'

Dr Labrador's response: 'Mr Inwood was in good health.'

Comment of Prosecution: 'So Mr Inwood why all the lies?'

'James Inwood chokes back dry tears,' Press comment.

Testimony of James' uncle, father's side, recorded during infamous trial: 'He kept assuring us he'd made a hundred per cent safe bets with our savings and to think all that time we were being played like fools and what with my wife getting ill at that time.' (To James) 'James Inwood you're a disgrace.'

'James calls out to his dead father, "Father father," chokes back dry tears,' Press comment.

James' journal submitted as evidence during infamous trial: 'Must escape what have I done.'

Evidence of Sadie Jestice, Inwood's lover submitted as evidence during infamous trial: 'The meeting at Windsor Great Park was awful. I wanted to look at his accounts having entrusted him with considerable sums he said he was was in the red I realised that he'd made use of it for his own purposes I said he was a thief he tried to strangle me then apologised.'

Evidence of Mr Madden, architect given during infamous trial: 'Mr Inwood said he wanted a house made of wood for himself and family full of life he said with an olde worlde feel.'

8

NARRATOR comments on the photo.

NARRATOR: 'The Lounge,' photographed by James Inwood.

Audience may or may not see the photo.

The room is divided into diverse separately functioning zones. On a dais the living-room dominated by free-standing chimney structure copper hood and dual-layered conduit parquet beech floor stripped pine panelled walls attached by tongue and groove to an exposed wood lattice on arbour side French windows full drop velveteen drapes held by swags (details supplied by Mr Madden architect) on the rear wall shelving numerous *objets* Stars and Stripe Russian nested dolls tiny opalescent pebbles midi-hifi stack brown buck-leather settee in front of open hearth with yucca plant dining room opening onto kitchen area floored with ceramic tiles long wooden table with pine chairs further on two Lloyd-loom chairs facing in separated by coffee table high vaulted ceiling of about one hundred square metres.

9

NARRATOR: Testimony of Claire's Mother. Recorded during infamous trial: 'I rang the alarm bell over and over again to no avail we trusted him with our savings in good faith but I asked myself what if he just pockets the lot.'

10

NARRATOR: Testimony of Inwood's uncle father's side. Recorded during infamous trial: 'He said he'd invested our savings and we'd reap real dividends and then time went by and we said to him come on then James what about these dividends you mentioned and he assured it was all coming good telling us he'd invested the money up in the City which'd be to our advantage we were completely at his mercy.' (To Inwood) 'James Inwood you are a disgrace.'

11

NARRATOR comments on a photo.

NARRATOR: 'The Barbecue,' photographed by James Inwood.

Audience may or may not see the photo.

L-shaped on the shorter arm sink and storage capacity on the longer stone work surface aromatic barbecue herbs to hand cost of construction, two thousand pounds VAT inclusive.

12

NARRATOR: James' vision: 'I see my parents eating beans on toast and suddenly they drop dead.' Recorded during infamous trial.

James' journal, extract read out and discussed during infamous trial: 'Love swells in me yes that really captures fully this feeling of love we just do what feels natural that phrase's good as well I feel this house is the perfect setting for our adventure mirroring back to us our harmony I never dreamed a place could do this talking back to us about our lives making us visible as creatures graced with memory and hope living careless of death in this unique home almost by accident having changed the very motion of time itself having framed fresh customs and rules that shield us immersed in the pleasure of everyday life the simplest gestures full of enduring freshness and force all thanks to an inescapable harmony as if the design's perfection lifted us up high suddenly simply idling from room to room getting in and out of chairs feels miraculous as if we have come out of convalescence into health.'

The Fall by Albert Camus: extracts copied out by James Inwood: 'For a while from the outside my life continued as if nothing had changed, I was on track and I rattled forward. As if on purpose, I was showered with praise. You know of course that's the first sign of danger: when men speak well of you you're in trouble. I was in trouble. And the engine started playing up suddenly grinding to a halt without apparent reason.'

'The slaughter of truth makes me dizzy.'

13

NARRATOR comments on a photo.

NARRATOR: 'The Swimming Pool,' photographed by James Inwood.

Audience may or may not see the photo.

Echoing the overall design concept with its kidney-bean shape seven metres long sunk in concrete building costs, 78 500, inclusive of VAT.

14

NARRATOR: James' journal, read out during infamous trial: 'After hesitating over my orchard finally settle for Braeburns red firm and uniform in colour. Advice given in Geoff Hamilton's catalogue: "Prior to planting soak your roots in a compound of soil and water. This little trick helps the tree bed down in the earth. Keep it well-watered at all times – the soil must be moist – and prune the tree in Summer, the growth season. You'll find this'll improve your fruit yield." '

15

NARRATOR: Letter from James Inwood to his lover Sadie Jestice submitted as evidence during infamous trial: 'Darling I'm losing control I consider the words of Okakura Kakuzo: "The void is all powerful for all is contained therein. In the void the only possibility is motion." '

Question from Prosecution to Sadie Jestice: 'He strangled you at Windsor Great Park?'

Answer of Sadie Jestice: 'He attempted to strangle me at Windsor Great Park.' Comments recorded during course of infamous trial.

16

NARRATOR: Extract from statement of Expert Witness submitted during infamous trial: 'Ensnared in deceit feeling encircled he constructs a system fabricates illnesses incapable of dealing with reality or surmounting obstacles he therefore represses them his entire life becoming reduced to a series of desperate evasions.'

Family photos published at the time of the notorious incident.

Audience may or may not see the photos.

Photo One: James round face good-natured mien medium-sized suit and tie.

Photo Two: Claire chestnut hair pale smile slightly frail skirt-suit and small hat painted nails.

Photo Three: Charlotte crew-neck pony-tailed the image of her father.

Photo Four: Timothy nicknamed Timmy apple-cheeked pale smile the image of his mother.

Article from the local paper: 'Eleventh January quintuple murder in Chepstow district armed man in cagoule breaks into Dr Inwood's manor grabs rolling-pin kills Inwood's wife goes upstairs slaughters their two children with .twenty-two rifle then evil work complete gets into car probably Nissan Namura speeds on a further three miles to slaughter same Inwood's parents with .twenty-two rifle Detective Inspector's remark: "There's something fishy about all this." '

Testimony of Sadie Jestice, James Inwood's mistress, recorded during infamous trial: 'When I worked out that the ninety thousand I'd trusted him with had gone up in smoke I was anxious to say the least but then when he came up with a cheque for forty thousand and then another one for twenty thousand claiming to have hit the jackpot I wasn't about to ask any questions even though I knew it was all lies.'

Evidence of Claire's mother recorded during infamous trial: 'My son-in-law who was overseeing the construction work and bankrupt killed my husband when he was up in the attic with my son-in-law my husband gave out a cry as my son-in-law pushed my husband down the stairs or so it seemed to me my son-in-law however told me my husband had slipped and when my son-in-law sold off our house following my husband's death I refused to stay with them and then when various large cheques went missing I realised the extent to which my son-in-law had swindled me.'

Comment of Prosecution recorded during infamous trial: 'Inwood your blind destructive rages are the product of an impenetrable narcissism – the problem in a nutshell.'

17

NARRATOR: Testimony of Anthony Bennett, librarian at the Wellcome Institute London, recorded during infamous trial: 'Mr Inwood would come to the library mainly in afternoons and quietly look up the specialist journals take some notes and leave he was a regular.'

18

NARRATOR: Headline of local paper: 'Tell us the Truth Dr Inwood.' Image depicts: Inwood eyes shut look of defeat policeman at side arms folded.

Audience may or may not see image.

19

NARRATOR: Testimony of Anthony Bennett, librarian at the Wellcome Institute London, recorded during infamous trial: 'One day Mr Inwood asked me out of the blue as to whether I had found my calling. I didn't know what to say so he rephrased the question saying

Are you doing the job you really want I said I was a temporary covering a maternity leave he said he was very low so to reciprocate I asked him if he was happy in his line of work and he replied that it met his requirements.'

NARRATOR comments on a photo.

'The Garden,' photographed by James Inwood.

Audience may or may not see the image.

The garden offers a unique configuration of acanthus aborescent lupins fennel poppies gorse and a camomile lawn sporting soft leafage known as 'heart's-ease'.

20

NARRATOR: Evidence of Anthony Bennett, librarian at the Wellcome Institute, London recorded during infamous trial: 'Mr Inwood seemed to me to be working to a sort of fantasy schedule one day I put this to him and he asserted that he was an international functionary working flexi-time that's what he said I asked what he did exactly and he had a sneezing fit which led to a bit of business with tissues.'

21

NARRATOR: Extract from article in local paper: 'Thirteenth January for generations the Inwoods have supplied this area with parish councillors and civil engineers Andrew the father being the best known his son James after taking his A levels sat medical school preliminary exams failed them and tried again resitting his second year no less than twelve times whilst at the same time raising a family and deceiving all about him until his cover was broken.'

22

NARRATOR: Evidence of Claire's mother. Recorded during infamous trial: 'It was after I recalled a debt contracted by my son-in-law to my husband of about ten thousand and my husband had mentioned the sum and my son-in-law had claimed his account was in the red and asked for patience it was after that point that they went up to the attic and my son-in-law pushed my husband down the stairs or so it seemed to me and like a nitwit I let him oversee selling the house as I didn't want anything to do with the sale of that house after my husband died I wouldn't abide in that house.'

23

NARRATOR: Evidence of Anthony Bennett, librarian at the Wellcome Institute, London, recorded during infamous trial. 'I checked through our database of international medical functionaries and he didn't feature there and when I probed him on this he told me he worked for some company based in Bahrain.'

NARRATOR comments on the photos.

Family photos.

Audience may or may not see the photos.

Photo One: Andrew the Father open gaze casual jersey walking boots fixed grin spectacles.

Photo Two: Alison the Mother tight perm crimson blouse patterned skirt spectacles.

24

NARRATOR: Testimony of Anthony Bennett librarian at the Wellcome Institute, London, recorded during infamous trial: 'I made some enquiries about this firm in Bahrain it turned out to be non-existent yet Inwood always appeared to be doing alright he drove a BMW looked pretty middle-class keeping his guard up as I watched him.'

25

NARRATOR comments on the photo.

NARRATOR: 'The Pergola,' photographed by James Inwood.

Audience may or may not see the image.

Festooned with vines gathered around the cosy enclosed interior its chestnutwood trellis accommodates intermingling clematis and rose the whole complete with duckboard flooring.

26

NARRATOR: Testimony of Anthony Bennett, librarian at Wellcome Institute London, recorded during infamous trial: 'One day Inwood told me he had cancer of the blood and I didn't see him for some time after that and then he turned up again claiming he was completely cured.'

27

NARRATOR: James Inwood's journal. Submitted as
evidence during infamous trial. 'In the woods find
solace sometimes scream and feel release at all times
drowning in an unfathomable pain that swallows
everything in darkness and burns insides yesterday
called on Dad who's as strong as an oak as per normal
asked me how I'm doing of course inside in agony but
being professional hypocrite hide it from him love
mother and father so much.'

28

NARRATOR comments on the photo.

NARRATOR: 'The Boundary Hedgerow,' photographed
by James Inwood.

Audience may or may not see the photo.

A double hedge comprising variegated privet spruce
and buddleia the whole contrastive and brilliant.

29

NARRATOR: Testimony of Anthony Bennett, librarian at
Wellcome Institute, London, recorded during infamous
trial: 'As I'd rumbled Inwood's game I awaited the
dénouement which I sensed would be special.'

30

NARRATOR: James Inwood's journal. Submitted as
evidence during infamous trial: 'Palm tree is dead

despite having carefully softened earth adding compound slow-action fertilisers to soil and copious watering death of palm tree has weakened powers of resistance yes.'

31

NARRATOR: Letter from Claire addressed to her friend Annie Roebuck. Submitted as evidence during infamous trial: 'June 1974 I am going to marry James I asked him if us being cousins was a problem he told me not to give it another thought we were cousins by marriage not blood ever since we've known each other James has tended to treat me like a sister isn't that weird he smiles all the time this smile worries me why does he smile he's failed his exams he's shown me his designs for the Manor it's going to be rather flash I'm planning to study pharmacology.'

Evidence of Annie Roebuck recorded during infamous trial: 'James was always smiling and her too smiling for no reason just this smiling couple it was almost boring I think they got on okay they loved their kids they were what you call happy folk they behaved like happy folk James went white as a ghost one evening when Claire whispered to me Annie something's the matter with James and he heard us I swear he heard us.'

32

NARRATOR: Testimony of Claire's mother recorded during infamous trial: 'One evening he slipped up during dinner he said yesterday I was at the office at the Wellcome Institute he said he had this office at the

Wellcome Institute but I'd seen him walking in the woods I was gathering kindling and I spotted him absolutely lost in his thoughts oblivious to me so that evening I said to myself you're a fraud and from that moment on I had premonitions.'

33

NARRATOR: Testimony of Annie Roebuck recorded during infamous trial: 'The week after Claire showed me a photo of James and she said if someone said James was a Soviet spy I'd believe them that's exactly what she said.'

34

NARRATOR: Testimony of Anthony Bennett, librarian at the Wellcome Institute, London, recorded during the infamous trial: 'When the scandal came to light and it was all over the papers I knew I'd been on the right lines I said to my colleague Terry Point I told you the bloke in the BMW was up to no good now do you believe me.'

35

NARRATOR: Extract from article in local paper: 'Twelfth January, Firemen were busy through the night of the tenth at the site of a house in flames at Brockwell four bodies were found inside three dead one unconscious police at the scene determined causes of death as not the fire but the impact of bullets from a .twenty-two rifle the police are on the case.'

36

NARRATOR: Testimony of Sadie Jestice, lover of James
Inwood, recorded during infamous trial: 'James and I
went on lovely excursions Rome St Petersburg he loved
changing scenery sunsets he was terribly sensitive I
trusted him totally.'

37

NARRATOR: Testimony of Claire's mother recorded
during infamous trial: 'I had this recurring dream that
he set fire to the house.'

Question from Defence: 'Did you mention this to those
nearest to you?'

Response of mother: 'The people nearest me would
have laughed in my face.'

38

NARRATOR: Letter from James Inwood to his parents
submitted as evidence during infamous trial: 'Bath 1972
Dear Dad and Mum life passes pretty uneventfully I'm
not wasting time often I sit and watch the Avon flow
Bath is pretty I'm so grateful that you let me opt for
Medicine over managing the stud farm though I miss
the woods and the paddock so much I think about you
loads and love you with all my heart.'

39

NARRATOR: Extract from letter of James to his parents
submitted as evidence during infamous trial: 'Bath 1972

I'm twenty years old and great things lie ahead of me I'm on the road to riches and Claire's studying pharmacology.'

40

NARRATOR: Testimony of Annie Roebuck recorded during infamous trial: 'Just before the events she said to me I think I'm starting to get it I said don't tell me James is a Soviet spy she said I don't want to say and when I pressed her she said her whole life was a lie I said what the hell do you mean she said to think he's mad to think I've married a ghost that's exactly how she put it.'

41

NARRATOR: Prosecution: 'What did you do all that time?'

Accused: 'Drove about.'

Judge: 'You drove about for twenty years?'

Accused: 'Yes yes.'

Prosecutor: 'And who paid for it all your wife your wife's family your parents your lover?'

Accused: 'Yes yes.'

42

NARRATOR: Testimony of Claire's mother. Recorded during infamous trial: 'One day I read him a proverb from Isaiah: "And you will blush for the gardens wherein you seek your pleasures." He couldn't take that he shouted and I shouted too and my daughter Claire and the children were all crying and he had tears in his eyes too and I quoted Isaiah again: "For destruction awaits all the transgressors and the sinners." Then he said to me you lot and your puny narrow lives then he went quiet and everyone went to bed.'

43

NARRATOR comments on the photo.

NARRATOR: 'The Summerhouse,' photographed by James Inwood.

Audience may or may not see the photo

Palisaded on a podium of chestnut wood hazel branches intermingling with vivacious aromatic herbiage in a nest of velvet-like sage yarrow and geraniums.

44

NARRATOR: Article published in Welsh language paper: 'Eleventh January Three Bodies Found three corpses have been discovered in the charred ruins of a manor just over the English border and two more in another house close by victims of savage murder spree or crime of passion? police are investigating whether bullets caused the fatalities one of the victims was a young woman her skull smashed in with a rolling pin.'

Article published in *The Telegraph*: 'Thirteenth January The Inwood Affair Under police interrogation James Inwood admits being present at the murder of his wife who was battered to death with a rolling pin:

'Two men in cagoules came in and killed her.'
'And you didn't try to defend her?'
'No my only crime is cowardice.'
After making this unconvincing statement James
Inwood was taken to the police station.'

45

NARRATOR: James's journal. Submitted as evidence
during infamous trial: 'Tenth January watched
documentary on Amazonian ants can't stop pissing
nothing will ever be the same again chaos in the
kitchen at no point did I shed tears no tears no legs
can't feel my legs my eyes shut drank coffee all the way
back from Windsor all comes back to you horrible can
smell the smell of the woods oh what have you done
look at my dead ones God blood on them my little
ones one day my life crashed can't say that unsayable
saying want to go to bed but Claire's here not very
sexy years you've been in hell my Claire my Charlie
my Timmy my dad my mum here invisible here haunt
me smells of death in here going to burn this book now
let the flames know – four a.m. be there with you any
minute now.'

46

NARRATOR: Article from local paper: 'Fifteenth January
I can't face this life declared James Inwood after
slaughtering his wife children and parents and after
speeding up the M4 to Windsor to try and finish off his
lover Sadie Jestice who managed to escape him with
this setback he fled back to his home in the Forest of
Dean and watched TV in his made-to-measure Manor

house with three dead bodies nearby he wrote his
journal took some barbiturates and set the house alight
the alarm was given out by the dustbinmen.'

47

NARRATOR: Letter from Sadie Jestice, James Inwood's
    lover. Published in the aftermath of the infamous trial:
    'In 1996 after the meeting at Windsor when you
    attacked me with tear-gas I hated you I wasn't aware
    until then that hatred could fill up all available space
    today when I think back to then I get this weird feeling
    of unrealness which infects everything I do or say I
    open a door and it feels bizarre I talk to my neighbour
    and afterwards wonder whether we really talked I'm
    broken in half and I have to admit it bereft of you you
    who led me to believe that life could be weightless.'